Adorable Creepy Monsters

Coloring Book

This Book Belongs To

Welcome To A World Where Nothing Makes Sense!

Free your thoughts! Explore and express your creativity with these illustrations. Nothing makes sense here. **WE ARE SERIOUS ABOUT THAT.** Even our name is random. So don't overthink it. Have fun and color your stress away!

Best Practices

Amazon's selection of paper is best suited for coloring pencils and alcohol-based markers. Wet mediums are advised to be accompanied by a sheet of paper behind the pages you are coloring to avoid any bleed-through that may occur.

Copyright © 2023 by A SPACE COWBOY

All Rights Reserved

No part of this book may be reproduced by any means (electronic, mechanical, including photocopy) without written permission from the publisher, except in the case of brief quotations embodied in articles and reviews. Sharing your colored pages online is allowed as long as it's not for profit.

ISBN: 9798386151881

Color Testing Page

READY TO SHARE?

Thank you for choosing and purchasing this book. We hope you had a great time coloring these pages. And let your random ideas flow.

Remember, they don't have to make sense.

That said, if you enjoyed this book, please don't hesitate to **SHARE** your colored pages, or **REVIEW** this book. It will also help us reach more coloring enthusiasts like you.

To leave us an honest review on Amazon, simply scan the code below.

US AMAZON LINK

UK AMAZON LINK

BUT WAIT! THERE IS A BONUS

Scan the code below, and you can sign up for our newsletter for updates on future releases, advance printable copies, and free bonus coloring pages right away!

SCAN ME

MORE FAN FAVORITE

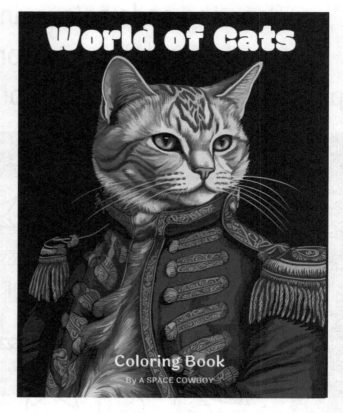

SCAN ME

SCAN ME

Made in United States
Troutdale, OR
09/30/2024

23273258R00060